STO√

P9-DZA-267

HOLIDAY COLLECTION

1/98

√

A Child's Story of Christmas

Illustrated by
Karin Williams

Based upon the Scriptures
Matthew 1:18–2:18
Luke 1:26–56; 2:1–40

Ideals Children's Books • Nashville, Tennessee
an imprint of Hambleton-Hill Publishing, Inc.

ISBN 1-57102-117-5

Library of Congress Card Catalog #97-5876
Library of Congress Cataloging-in-Publication Data is available.

In the sixth month, God sent the angel Gabriel to the city of Nazareth, which was in the land of Galilee.

Gabriel went to the home of a young girl named Mary. When he found her, he said, "Greetings, you who are most highly favored. The Lord is with you."

Mary was frightened by the angel and his words. Seeing her fear, Gabriel said to her gently, "Do not be afraid, Mary, for you have found favor with God. You will bear a son and you are to name him Jesus. He will be called the Son of the Highest, and the Lord will give him a kingdom that will never end."

"How can I have a son when I'm not yet married?" asked Mary in confusion.

"The power of the Holy Spirit will overshadow you, so that the child will be the Son of God," Gabriel answered. "Even now your cousin Elizabeth, who was once barren, is going to have a son in her old age. For with God, nothing is impossible."

Mary's eyes widened with wonder, and she whispered, "Let it be as you have said."

Gabriel left, and Mary sat down to ponder all that he had told her.

Then, remembering what the angel had said about Elizabeth, Mary gathered some things together and hurried to the hill country to see her cousin.

As Mary walked up to Elizabeth's house, she called out to her. At the sound of her cousin's voice, Elizabeth was filled with the Holy Spirit. Hurrying to greet Mary, she said, "Blessed are you among women, and blessed is the child you will bear. As soon as I heard your voice, my own baby leapt for joy inside my womb."

Mary's heart was filled with happiness and she replied, "My spirit glorifies God my Savior, for he has remembered me, his humble servant. From this time on, all generations will call me blessed."

Mary stayed with her cousin for about three months, and then she returned home.

Mary was engaged to a man named Joseph, who was a carpenter. But before they were married, Mary was found to be with child. When Joseph heard the news, he was confused and upset.

But Joseph was a kind man, and he did not want to publicly shame Mary. He decided to end their engagement quietly.

Then, the angel of the Lord appeared to him in a dream and said, "Joseph, do not be afraid to take Mary as your wife. The child she carries is the child of the Lord. She will bear a son. You will call him Jesus, which means 'the Lord saves,' for he will save the people from their sins."

Joseph awoke and, just as the angel had told him to do, he took Mary home as his wife.

During those same days, Caesar Augustus ordered that all the known world be taxed. Everyone had to return to his own city to be counted.

Since Joseph was a descendant of the house of David, he had to go to the city of David, which was called Bethlehem. He took Mary with him, and together they traveled from Nazareth up through Galilee to Bethlehem.

Because Mary was great with child, she and Joseph traveled slowly. It was late when they arrived in Bethlehem, and the city was crowded with others who had also come to be counted. They searched for a place to spend the night, but there was no room at the inn. Finally, they found shelter among the animals in a stable.

While they rested there, Mary's son was born. Having nothing else, she wrapped the baby in swaddling clothes and gently laid him in a manger. And, as they had been told by the angels, they named the baby Jesus.

On that same night, a group of shepherds were gathered in a nearby field, keeping watch over their flock through the night.

The angel of the Lord appeared before them, with the glory of God shining all around him. The shepherds were frightened.

"Do not be afraid," said the angel. "I bring you news of great joy for all people. This day, in the city of David, a Savior is born, who is Christ the Lord. This will be a sign to you: You will find the baby wrapped in swaddling clothes and lying in a manger."

Suddenly the sky was filled with angels. They praised God and said,

Glory to God in the highest,
and on earth, peace and good will toward men.

After the angels had returned to heaven, the shepherds said to each other, "Let us go to Bethlehem and see this baby that the Lord has told us about."

The shepherds hurried toward Bethlehem, running and stumbling in the darkness. At last they reached the stable where they found Mary and Joseph. And next to them was the baby Jesus, lying in the manger, just as the angels had said.

Having seen the child, the shepherds ran out into the night, praising God and telling all who would listen of the wonderful things they had seen and heard.

Mary watched and listened to all that was happening around her. She remembered all these things and studied them in her heart.

Eight days passed, and the time came for Jesus to be taken to the Temple. There he would be presented to the Lord, as was the custom.

At the Temple that day, there was an old man named Simeon. He had been told by the Holy Ghost that he would not die until he had seen the Christ. When Mary and Joseph brought Jesus into the Temple, Simeon rushed over to them. He took the child in his arms, and praising God he said, "Now I can die in peace, for I have seen your salvation."

Joseph and Mary were amazed by Simeon's words. As they were pondering them, a prophetess named Anna came up to them also. Anna was a widow who lived in the Temple, serving God night and day with fastings and prayers. Seeing the baby Jesus, she too began praising God and declaring that this was the child who would save all of Israel from its sins.

When Mary and Joseph had fulfilled all the customs, they returned to their own city.

Now, Jesus was born during the time of King Herod, who was a terribly wicked ruler.

One day, wise men came from the east to see King Herod. Not knowing of Herod's wickedness, they asked, "Where is the child who was born King of the Jews? We have seen his star and have come to worship him."

When Herod heard this, he hurried out of the room. The thought that there might be another king in his kingdom made him furious.

Herod quickly gathered together the chief priests and scribes and demanded that they tell him where the Christ child had been born.

They studied their scrolls and then came back with an answer: "Bethlehem."

Herod did not want the wise men to know of his evil plans, so he went to them and said, "Search for the child in the city of Bethlehem. When you have found him, bring me word, so that I may go and worship him also," Herod lied.

So the wise men left for Bethlehem.

The wise men followed the star, which went before them, until it stood over the place where the young child was.

Rejoicing, the wise men went into the house. When they saw the young child with Mary, they fell down and worshiped him. Opening up their packs, they presented him with gifts of gold and frankincense and myrrh.

Then, being warned by God in a dream that they should not return to Herod, they left for their own country by a different route.

After the wise men had left, the angel of the Lord again appeared to Joseph in a dream.

"Take the child and his mother and go to Egypt," the angel told Joseph. "Stay there until I send word, for King Herod will try to kill the child."

Joseph arose quickly and woke Mary. Though it was the middle
of the night, they bundled up the sleeping child and fled to Egypt.
There they stayed until the death of King Herod.

The years passed, and Jesus grew into a man. As the Son of God, he gave to the world many wonderful gifts. Then, through his own death and resurrection, Jesus gave to mankind the greatest gifts of all—salvation from sin and the promise of everlasting life for all who believe.

And for this reason, each year at Christmas, we celebrate the birth of our Savior: Jesus Christ.